Your

New

Beginning

STEP

TWO

Your

New

beginning

PART

TWO

Your

New

Beginning

STEP

TWO

by
Dr. Willie J. Malone

Printed by

The Overmountain Press

JOHNSON CITY, TENNESSEE

Your New Beginning
STEP TWO
ISBN 0-88144-008-6
Copyright © by Dr. Willie J. Malone
Abundant Living
260 Victory Lane
Kingsport, Tennessee 37664

1992 Fourth Printing by The Overmountain Press

Contents

"If you want to win don't quit."

— Dr. Willie J. Malone

Preface

I am pastor of an interdenominational church in Kingsport, Tennessee and an optometrist. My primary purpose in writing this book is to provide a basis for your spiritual growth as well as to share my personal experiences as a pastor, businessman, husband and father.

Amway is not a Christian corporation. It is a beautiful business which offers an opportunity to change the course of one's life, to realize dreams, and the freedom to accomplish goals once thought impossible. I believe in this business.

Contrary to some religious thinking, people in Amway are not "using God to make money." God does not mind if you are successful. He desires it! He will do anything He said He would do to make you successful, IF you follow His guidelines. The Bible is the greatest "HOW TO SUCCEED" book ever written. However, God has given every human being the right to choose his own destiny. You must choose yours. I was not born an optometrist. My birth announcement did not read: "Mrs. A.C. Malone gave birth to an eight-pound, six-ounce optometrist." I chose to be an eye doctor. I chose to be an Amway distributor. I chose to be a Christian. You have the same freedom of choice in life. I believe you make hundreds of decisions every day. Success or failure will depend upon the accuracy of those decisions. Therefore, as a minister and businessman, I rely on the wisdom of God to help me make those decisions. I realize that I am very limited within myself. But with God as my partner, I am unlimited because He is unlimited.

As you read this book you will understand a minister's love for people. You will identify the corresponding love and enthusiasm you experience when you see someone succeed because you cared enough to share with him. I enjoy praying for those people whom we have sponsored in Amway and for our very own sponsor. Every day I make intercessory prayer for the people I will come in contact with that day. I also pray for my friends and for those who have helped me in my business. I believe that this intercessory prayer has changed my entire business life. When you begin to get involved in this type of prayer, your business will grow beyond the realm of your natural mind.

It thrills me to see so many people come forward in our Sunday morning meetings and accept Jesus Christ as their Lord. My greatest concern, however, is what they will do when they get back home. That is why I have written this book. May God richly bless you as you prepare now to take STEP TWO. I love you.

Introduction

On July 11, 1982, a beautiful Sunday morning, in Denver, Colorado, in a meeting of Amway distributors, Dr. Theron Nelson gave the invitation for those who would like to make a committment to Jesus Christ and to become born-again Christians. He handed the microphone to me. A miracle was about to take place. Nearly one thousand of those Amway distributors repeated the prayer of repentance and asked Jesus Christ into their lives. What a thrill! The entire weekend had been electrifying, but this moment was the icing on the cake. The overwhelming display of God's love shown through the marvelous leadership was a sight to behold. Those in attendance were watching their business partners make one of the greatest decisions in their lives.

After the service a young man from Minnesota came up to me and asked: "What's next?"; "What do I do now?" I shared briefly with him and my religious head wanted to tell him to go back home and go to church. However, the Spirit of God on the inside of me would not allow me to say that. I knew how important going to church was, but that was not the answer to his questions. As I prayed and asked God for the right answer, He instructed me to sit down and write it in the form of a book. So, in obedience, I have done what He told Jeremiah in the Old Testament to do:

The word that came to Jeremiah from the Lord, saying,

Thus speaketh the Lord God of Israel, saying, WRITE THEE ALL THE WORDS THAT I HAVE SPOKEN UNTO THEE IN A BOOK.

Jeremiah 30:1-2

Since step one was making the decision to serve Jesus Christ, *STEP TWO* will answer your question, "What do I do now?'' I believe the information you presently have in your possession will cause you to grow spiritually and keep you from being weary and discouraged in the days ahead. Please do not think for one minute that we can reduce our daily living to a formula and that everything will be perfect. It takes time to grow. As you read *STEP TWO* you will find guidelines to successful Christian living. You are going to learn how to live the complete life, one filled with happiness and excitement. Sound great? It is!

Now that you belong to the Kingdom of God, you are unstoppable. But do not expect to be a spiritual giant overnight. Just as it takes time for your business to grow, it will take time for your Christian growth. Be patient. Take the time to read this book more than once. You will discover what every truly successful Christian has discovered: WHEN YOU HAVE GOD ON YOUR TEAM YOU ARE A WINNER IN LIFE. All right, winner, let's find out WHAT'S NEXT.

1

What Happened?

When you confessed the Lord Jesus Christ as your personal Savior and Lord and prayed the prayer of faith, according to Romans 10:9-10 you were born again, spiritually born into the Kingdom of God. Jesus tells us in John 3:3: *Verily, verily, I say unto thee, except a man be born again, he cannot see the kingdom of God.* In that rebirth experience, you entered into a covenant relationship with Almighty God. Since His Word is that covenant, every promise in it now belongs to you. The best thing you can start doing today is to read your covenant and find out what rightfully belongs to you.

I have heard people say, "Well, I don't feel like I am a Christian." Your relationship with Jesus Christ is not based on feeling. A lady asked me one day, "Dr. Malone, do you ever feel like you are not a Christian?" No, because I have never been able to find in my covenant that my salvation is dependent upon my feelings. Nowhere does it say that I am saved if I **feel** like I am saved. Rather, I am saved because God says so in His Word. And God cannot lie.

Therefore if any man be in Christ, he is a new creature: old things are passed away; behold, all things are become new (2 Cor. 5:17). Do you know what that means? It means that you are a NEW CREATURE. One translation says that you are a new species. All the things you have done wrong in your life have passed away, are gone and buried, never to be held against you again. All things are now new! You are a new person in Christ Jesus. God has forgiven you of every sin, and He will never bring them to your remembrance or remind you of them again. Do not allow the devil to harass you about your past. Colossians 2:14 says that the handwriting of ordinances that was against you has been blotted out and nailed to the cross.

Also, you must learn to forgive yourself. *There is therefore now no condemnation to them which are in Christ Jesus* (Rom. 8:1). Just think, your slate is clean. Today is the first day of the rest of your life. Do you know why you feel so good and clean on the inside? Because the blood of Jesus has washed away every sin. Your spirit is now created in the image of Almighty God. You are in Him and He is in you. You and God are a team. You must now learn to listen to Him and follow His instructions.

For as many as are led by the Spirit of God, THEY ARE THE SONS OF GOD.

For ye have not received the spirit of bondage again to fear; but ye have received the Spirit of adoption, whereby we cry, Abba, Father.

The Spirit itself beareth witness with our spirit, THAT WE ARE THE CHILDREN OF GOD:

And if children, then HEIRS; HEIRS OF GOD, and JOINT-HEIRS WITH CHRIST; if so be that we suffer with him, that we may be also glorified together.

Romans 8:14-17

Notice that you are a son of God. You are a child of God and therefore are an heir of God and a joint-heir with Jesus Christ. That means that everything in the Kingdom of God belongs to you too. Everything that God has, you have a legal claim to. He desires to give you His blessings. He wants you to have your rightful inheritance. Jesus Christ went to the cross and suffered so that you would not have to suffer. He bore the stripes on His back for your healing. The chastisement of your peace was upon Him. (Is. 53:5.) He became poor that you might become rich. (2 Cor. 8:9.) You see, Jesus was your substitute at Calvary. What He did on the cross, He did for you so that you could go free. No longer do you have to bow your knee to circumstances. You can use God's Word and exercise your faith and rise above every storm in life. You can soar like an eagle over every difficulty and problem because your covenant grants you that right and power.

You can say with Phillipians 4:13: *I can do ALL THINGS through Christ which strengtheneth me.*

Paul tells you in Philippians 4:19: *My God shall supply ALL YOUR NEED according to his riches in glory by Christ Jesus.*

You can agree with David: *The Lord is my shepherd; I shall not want* (Ps. 23:1).

And the Lord, speaking through John, assures you: *Beloved, I wish above all things that thou mayest prosper and be in health, even as thy soul prospereth* (3 John 2).

All of these are in your contract with God. They are powerful promises. They are yours.

Yes, you are now "born again" and belong to God. Today is the beginning of a new and exciting life that will lead you to heights that you never before thought possible. God is pleased with you. As a matter of fact, you can look at what has happened to you like this: GOD HAS JUST SPONSORED YOU INTO HIS BUSINESS. YOU ARE A PARTNER WITH GOD. HE IS YOUR MAIN UPLINE. LEARN TO LISTEN TO HIM. TAKE HIS ADVICE. DO WHAT HE SAYS TO DO. YOUR FUTURE IS BRIGHTER TODAY THAN IT EVER HAS BEEN BEFORE. Welcome Aboard, Partner.

*"The greatest gift you
can give to God
is Yourself"*

— Dr. Willie J. Malone

2

What Next?

You may have accepted Christ as your Savior in a meeting filled with excitement and enthusiasm. It was easy to believe when surrounded by others so full of faith. But then you must go back home and begin your new life alone. I must caution you at this point not to let the devil steal your joy.

Mark 4:15 says that Satan will come immediately to take away the Word that has been sown in your heart. You may go home and the thought may come to you: "I'm not really a Christian." Don't entertain that thought for a second! Never doubt your salvation experience. Romans 10:9-10 says that if you confess with your mouth the Lord Jesus Christ and believe in your heart that God has raised Him from the dead, then you shall be saved. It does not say: "If you confess with your mouth and believe in your heart, **and you can feel it,** you shall be saved." So tell the devil to take his lies and get off your case. Let him know that you know who you are in Christ Jesus and that no one can talk you out of it.

Say this aloud right now:

"I REFUSE TO ALLOW THE DEVIL TO STEAL THE WORD FROM ME. I HAVE ASKED JESUS TO COME INTO MY HEART AND HE IS IN ME. I AM THE RIGHTEOUSNESS OF GOD IN CHRIST JESUS. I AM A CHRISTIAN AND AM NOT ASHAMED OF IT. JESUS IS NOW THE ONLY LORD OF MY LIFE."

Next, you should begin to get better acquainted with your new friend, Jesus Christ. You might ask, "How do I do that?" Do you remember your first date with that special someone in your life? You went out together and in the course of time all kinds of questions were asked. You talked and listened, talked and listened until after a few weeks you were well acquainted and felt comfortable with each other. You knew what she (or he) liked and disliked. You knew what hurt her, what made her feel good. You knew what pleased her and displeased her. That relationship grew because you desired to be in her presence. That is the very principle that will cause you to grow spiritually. Take time to talk to God. Listen to Him. Read the Bible and find out how He operates. Discover what He likes and dislikes. Find out what pleases Him and displeases Him. Talk to Him in your own words. Don't try to impress Him with big words or fancy talk. Just talk to Him as you would talk to anyone else you love dearly.

It was a great revelation to me when I learned that I did not have to speak Elizabethan English when I talked to God. I was so glad to know that God could understand "Tennessee." Talk in you own words: "Good morning, God." "Jesus, I need some help." "Lord, what would You like for me to do for You today?" When you ask Him questions, be quiet for a while and allow Him to speak back to you. You probably will not hear an audible voice. But way down deep inside you there will be a small, still voice that you have referred to many times as a "hunch." Actually, you as a Christian will hear three voices: God's, Satan's, and your own. You must learn to distinguish and identify each one. As you mature, you will become much more accurate.

Everything you do should be checked with God's Word. If your plan agrees with God's Word, do it. If not, don't do it. If you are not certain, seek Godly counsel. You should begin right now to confess that you have the wisdom of God. James 1:5 says: *If any of you lack wisdom, let him ask of God, that giveth to all men liberally, and upbraideth not AND IT SHALL BE GIVEN HIM.* Don't allow yourself to say things like: "I just can't do anything right," or, "I am so dumb," or, "I can't remember anything." You can be hung by your tongue.

Proverbs 18:21 says that death and life are in the power of the tongue. James 3:10 declares that out of the mouth proceeds blessing and cursing. In Mark 11:23 Jesus told His disciples that whatever a person says with his mouth and believes in his heart, will come to pass. This can work for you or against you. Why? Because it is a spiritual law. As a new Christian, you should begin immediately to put this law to work FOR you. It is like the law of gravity. It will work whether you believe it or not. Remember: IF GOD'S WORD SAYS IT, BELIEVE IT, BECAUSE IT IS ALREADY SETTLED.

Studying the Bible

In studying the Bible there are no set patterns that will work every time for every person. There are some basic study habits that I have used and are enjoyable to me. First, you need to purchase a good Bible concordance like Strong's or Cruden's. If you want to do a word study on some subject such as healing or prosperity, look up the words and write down the scriptures and cross references. This is much better than just opening your Bible at random and reading wherever it opens. I have read the four Gospels — Matthew, Mark, Luke and John — with this thought in mind: "How did Jesus react in circumstances? What did He do when He was faced with trials and temptations?" When you learn what He did, pattern your life after Him. This is very important. Sometimes people will let you down and disappoint you. But if you pattern your life after Jesus, He will never disappoint you.

Another way I suggest you study the Bible is to read the Old Testament and correlate it with the New Testament. For example, the book of Joshua in the Old Covenant and the book of Ephesians in the New Covenant are almost direct parallels. Both of these are great faith building blocks.

You may desire to study the great men of the Bible individually. Also, there are 31 chapters in the book of Proverbs, so you could read one each day of the month. Avoid getting into trivia and wild goose chases. Take notes as you read. Mark in your Bible. Underline the key words and phrases and write in the margins. Above all things, always precede your study time with prayer.

Pray in this manner:

"LORD, HELP ME TO UNDERSTAND WHAT I AM ABOUT TO READ. I WANT TO LEARN YOUR WAYS AND TO WALK IN THEM. I WELCOME THE HOLY SPIRIT TO REVEAL TO ME THE GREAT TRUTHS IN YOUR WORD. AMEN."

Which Bible?

There are many translations of the Bible that are excellent. One of my favorites is *The Amplified Bible* by Zondervan. It gives the most detailed translation with everyday language that is easy to read. One of the easiest translations is *The Living Bible*. This version is very modern and written for ready understanding. Zondervan also publishes a *Layman's Parallel New Testament* which compares four popular translations in parallel columns. This is an excellent study Bible and would be very handy as you grow and study the Word. A very popular translation is the *New American Standard Bible*. However, I still lean heavily on the *King James Version*. Find the one that best suits you and with which you are most comfortable and use it.

One last very important bit of advice. Find time each day for your own private devotions. I have discovered the best time to study and pray is early in the morning before the busy schedule of the day. It sure makes the day better and more beautiful to start it off with prayer and study.

A good thing to do right now is to close your eyes and meditate about when you are going to read God's Word and pray. Then complete the following statement:

"FATHER, IN THE NAME OF JESUS, MY DESIRE IS TO STUDY YOUR WORD EACH DAY FOR _30_ MINUTES. I WILL TALK TO YOU DURING THIS SPECIAL TIME AND LEARN TO LISTEN TO YOU AS YOU TALK TO ME. MY BEST TIME IS _MORNING_ (morning, noon, evening, night)."

SIGNED _____

DATE _____8-4-9?_____

"After you pray take some time to be quiet and listen."

"When you talk to God in prayer, listen, he will talk to you."

"Prayer is more than just talking to God. Prayer includes listening. Learn the language of silence."

— Dr. Willie J. Malone

3

How to Pray Effectively

*And it came to pass, that, as he was praying in a certain place,
when he ceased, one of his disciples said unto him, Lord, TEACH
US TO PRAY, as John also taught his disciples.*

Luke 11:1

Ye ask, and receive not, BECAUSE YE ASK AMISS.

James 4:3

Prayer is the key that unlocks the door to the impossible.
For that reason, this will be the most important chapter in
this book. Read it carefully.

The disciples of Jesus Christ must have put a high
premium on the accuracy of prayer because they asked Jesus
to teach them how to pray. Many prayers go unanswered
because many Christians do not know how to pray according
to God's Word. If we are to reach the Throne of God we must
follow the rules He laid down in the Rulebook. One of the
most common errors people make when praying is asking
"for Jesus' sake." That phrase is never used in any prayer in
the Bible, and nowhere did our Lord ever instruct us to ask
God that anything be done "for His sake."

Another common mistake is praying "if it be Thy will."
We are going to shed some light on these areas and you will
be amazed at the results you see when you pray correctly.
After all, didn't James say that you ask but do not receive
because you ask incorrectly? Let's turn that around from the
negative to the positive: YOU ASK, AND RECEIVE,
BECAUSE YOU ASK CORRECTLY. Now let's learn to ask
correctly.

21

Ask in the Name of Jesus

And in that day ye shall ask me nothing. Verily, verily, I say unto you, WHATSOEVER YE SHALL ASK THE FATHER IN MY NAME, HE WILL GIVE IT YOU.
Hitherto have ye asked nothing IN MY NAME: ask, and ye shall receive, that your joy may be full.

John 16:23-24

So I suggest that you begin your next prayer in this fashion: "Father, in the Name of Jesus . . ." You must know that Jesus is our only approach to the Father. He is our Intercessor, our Mediator, our Power of Attorney. Jesus gave us the right to use His Name. In Matthew 28:18 He said: *All power is given unto me in heaven and in earth.* And then He turned around and gave that power to the believers.

Jesus told us to ask and that we would receive so that our joy would be full. You cannot be full of joy if you are poor, sick and depressed. Begin to use the Name of Jesus to break Satan's power over your finances, your body, your mind. Here is a good way to pray correctly concerning a stronghold in your life:

"IN THE NAME OF JESUS CHRIST OF NAZARETH, DEVIL, I BIND YOU FROM MY FINANCES, MY BODY, MY MIND. I CLAIM DELIVERANCE IN THE NAME OF THE LORD JESUS CHRIST."

By so doing, you just broke the enemy's power over those areas in your life. Do not allow yourself to be tempted into thinking about those things again. If the devil can hold you in the thought arena, he will defeat you. But if you hold him in the faith arena, you will whip him. Just DO NOT LET HIM GET YOU TO THINKING ABOUT THE PROBLEM! When you learn to operate like that, you will have joy in your life.

Christians should be joyful all the time, even in the midst of trials and temptations. You might say: "Well, I thought God put us through trials and tests to make us stronger and to draw us closer to Him." You may get

22

stronger and closer to God when you go through a trial, but let me set the record straight right now. GOD DOES NOT TRY YOU NOR TEST YOU. HE ALREADY KNOWS YOUR HEART. The trying and testing comes from the devil. He wants to steal the Word and the joy that was sown in your heart. When you begin to stand on God's Word and to confess, "I believe that Jesus meets all my needs; Jesus is the Lord of my life; I can do all things through Christ," you suddenly become very dangerous to Satan. He knows he must stop you from saying those things. So he brings trials and temptations against you to try to shake your faith and to get you to give up. But James says that if you will resist the devil and stand your ground, he will flee. But you must know how to resist him. Sometimes you need help.

In Matthew 18:19 Jesus told His disciples: *Again I say unto you, That if TWO of you shall agree on earth as touching any thing that they shall ask, it shall be done for them of my Father which is in heaven.* There will be times in the days ahead when you will need someone to agree with you in prayer. If you are married, the best prayer partner you could possibly have is your mate. Join hands and ask God to meet your need according to His riches in glory. (Phil. 4:19.) If you ask for something and it doesn't manifest itself right away, do not give up! Keep your faith working for you and believe God will do what He said He would do. AND HE WILL! You see, you are mighty in prayer. But you can be mightier with someone else joining you.

The Prayer of Faith

We have a part to play in praying. First, of course, we must ask. Then we must say it, agree on it, believe in our heart, and then receive it. You should become very familiar with these five scriptures:

I. Mark 11:24:

Therefore I say unto you, What THINGS soever ye desire, when ye pray, believe that ye receive them, and ye shall have them.

II. James 5:15:

And the PRAYER OF FAITH shall save the sick, and the Lord shall raise him up; and if he have committed sins, they shall be forgiven him.

III. Hebrews 11:1:

Now faith is the substance of things hoped for, the evidence of things NOT SEEN.

IV. Second Corinthians 4:18:

While we look not at the THINGS which are seen, but at the THINGS which are not seen: for the THINGS which are seen are temporal; but the THINGS which are not seen are eternal.

V. Romans 4:17:

(As it is written, I have made thee a father of many nations,) before him whom he believed, even God, who quickeneth the dead, AND CALLETH THOSE THINGS WHICH BE NOT AS THOUGH THEY WERE.

In all five of the above scriptures there are two comparable components: THINGS and NOT SEEN. The prayer of faith has to do with ''things'' and the ''not seen'' realm. If you don't believe that you have received the things you prayed for until you have seen them with your eyes, then you are not operating in faith. Begin to believe that you have what you prayed for before you can actually see them. This will work in every area of your prayer life including the physical, spiritual, financial, mental, social and material. Jesus said to believe that you receive **when you pray.** THAT IS FAITH. In the final analysis, it is **your faith** that determines the extent of your blessings.

Pray this prayer aloud right now:

''HEAVENLY FATHER, IN THE NAME OF JESUS, I MAKE THIS QUALITY DECISION: I WILL WALK BY FAITH AND NOT BY SIGHT. I AM A BELIEVER, NOT A DOUBTER. I ACCEPT YOUR WORD WITHOUT COMPROMISE. IT IS THE FINAL AUTHORITY IN MY LIFE. I SUBMIT TO YOU ON THIS _____ DAY OF _____, 19 __, THAT I WILL CALL THOSE

THINGS WHICH BE NOT AS THOUGH THEY WERE. I
WILL BELIEVE THAT I RECEIVE THE THINGS I ASK
FOR BEFORE I SEE THEM WITH MY EYES. I HAVE FULL
CONFIDENCE IN YOUR WORD, THAT YOU ARE
CAPABLE OF PERFORMING WHAT YOUR WORD SAYS.
YOU DESIRE TO GIVE GOOD GIFTS TO ME. I DESIRE
TO WALK IN YOUR TRUTH. WHEN I COME AGAINST
AN OBSTACLE, I WILL USE THE NAME OF JESUS TO
GET ME OVER IT EVERY TIME. THANK YOU FOR
GIVING ME THE RIGHT TO USE HIS NAME SO THAT I
CAN WALK IN VICTORY EVERY DAY. I BELIEVE IN
THE NAME OF JESUS. AMEN.''

The Armor of God

Finally, my brethren, BE STRONG IN THE LORD, and in the power of his might.

PUT ON THE WHOLE ARMOUR OF GOD, that ye may be able to stand against the wiles of the devil.

Ephesians 6:10-11

You are to be strong in the Lord. He told you how to do it — by putting on His armor so you can stand against the devil. But you do not put on this armor and say, "OK, Lord, I have on Your armor; now take care of me." No, God is not going to resist the devil, YOU are. Wear the HELMET OF SALVATION and the BREASTPLATE OF RIGHTEOUSNESS, gird your loins with TRUTH, shod your feet with the preparation of the GOSPEL OF PEACE, carry your SHIELD OF FAITH and wield the SWORD OF THE SPIRIT, which is the WORD OF GOD. (Eph. 6:13-17.) But YOU must use it, God won't do it for you.

Actually, there are two ways to wrestle against the principalities, powers, rulers of darkness and spiritual wickedness in high places:

1. By being clad in the armor of God (vs. 13-17.)
2. By praying with all kinds of prayers (v. 18.)

This armor is effective against every aspect of the devil's operation. It works in all areas of his trickery. We have complete power and supremacy over the enemy. But we must know where the fight is — it is in prayer.

Prayer unlocks the door to the impossible. Satan knows that in order to stop God from working for us, he has to stop us. How does he do that? He tries to build a barrier between us and God by deceiving us into thinking that our prayers are not working and that God is "holding out" on us. But once we have learned how to pray and how this armor works, Satan is whipped.

So, when you pray and believe, you are going to win the battle every time. I want you to think about this next statement: YOU WILL NEVER SUCCEED WITHOUT THE WORD OF GOD AND PRAYER. Somewhere down the line you will get beat. You may say: "Well, if it is God's will, I will succeed." No, that is not true! God's will is for **you** to succeed. If your will is to succeed, then you and God are in agreement and it shall come to pass. But if you do not exercise the faith God has given you, nothing will happen. **You** are the determining factor. **You** cast the deciding vote — by your actions.

Even then Satan will try to throw up obstacles. But whenever anything gets in the way of a faith man, he straps on his armor and uses the Name of Jesus to tear down that obstacle and march on to victory after victory.

Three Divisions of Prayer
  I. Prayer That Changes Things
 II. Prayer of Thanksgiving and Praise
III. Prayer of Dedication and Worship

It is vitally important to understand that there are divisions or differences in prayer. It is not enough just to pray, we must know the rules of prayer. If you get the prayer that changes things mixed up with the prayer of dedication and worship, it will not work. The rules are different. It is like trying to play basketball with a football. When it comes to prayer, most people just throw a bunch of words up in the air and hope it works. It won't. If you want to cross out your prayers, then break God's rules for praying. He won't come down and beat you over the head and say: "You missed it, you prayed to Me wrong." But neither will your prayers be answered. But there is no reason for any Christian to be ignorant about prayer. We have His Word and it clearly tells us HOW TO PRAY. So it is important to study the kinds of prayer and then to DO what you learn. Now let's look at each of these different types of prayers.

Prayer That Changes Things
There are four kinds of prayers that change things:
1. Prayer of agreement
2. Prayer of petition and supplication
3. Prayer of binding and loosing
4. Prayer of intercession

Prayer of Agreement
Again I tell you, if two of you on earth agree (harmonize together, together make a symphony) about — anything and everything — whatever they shall ask, it will come to pass and be done for them by My Father in heaven.

Matthew 18:19 AMP

Do not hesitate to ask another person to pray with you concerning your needs. Just be sure the other person is in agreement with you. If he is "hoping and praying" and you are praying and believing, the two of you are not in total agreement. Make sure your partner believes it will come to pass too. Be very selective in your choice of a prayer partner.

A lady called me one evening and asked me to agree with her in prayer concerning her finances. I shared some principles of God's Word with her and then asked: "Do you believe that God will meet your needs?"

She replied: "I don't know if He will or not. I sure hope He does."

I told her that we were not in agreement. After teaching her about what it means to agree on earth, I asked her again. This time she was sure God would meet her needs and we prayed and agreed according to Matthew 18:19, AND GOD MET HER NEEDS!!

Prayer of Petition and Supplication

Be careful for nothing; but in every thing by prayer and SUPPLICATION with thanksgiving let your requests be made known unto God.

Philippians 4:6

Petition and supplication actually mean a formal request made to a higher authority. Can you imagine walking into the office of the President of the United States not knowing one thing you wanted to talk to him about? Just walking in and sitting down to engage in idle chit-chat? He would ask you: "What can I do for you?" Suppose you just started jabbering, not making any sense at all, or crying, or yelling, or repeating the same words over and over again? What do you think would happen?

Well, to say the least, he would very likely wonder what you were doing there, wouldn't he? Before going in to meet with the President you would want to be prepared. You should make out a request. Do some research. Find out what he thinks about your proposal before you go in and then you will know what avenue to use to approach him. That would be the way to get results.

That is also the way to get results from God. Prepare a petition. Write it down. Work on it. Find out what His Word says about it. Fellowship with Jesus in prayer before going to God with it. You will always find God there waiting to meet your needs. There are going to be times you can see a need ahead, even before it happens. Petition God for it.

28

For this reason I am telling you, whatever you ask for in prayer, believe — trust and be confident — that it is granted to you, and you will [get it].

Mark 11:24 AMP

Note the word "granted" in the above scripture. That means it is a sure thing. Some years ago when I signed a grant-in-aid scholarship with East Tennessee State University to play college basketball, I knew all my college education was paid. I never doubted or worried if the university would pay for my books, food, tuition or board. I knew they would not fail. I also know that Jesus never fails. If you have a need in your life, petition God, write it down, tell Him and watch Him honor and grant your request.

Prayer of Binding and Loosing

Verily I say unto you, Whatsoever ye shall BIND on earth shall be BOUND in heaven: and whatsoever ye shall LOOSE on earth shall be LOOSED in heaven.

Matthew 18:18

The wicked spirits against which we operate are controlled when we bind them. When you go into a place and begin to feel unrestful in your spirit, begin to bind Satan immediately:

"SATAN, I BIND YOU FROM THIS PLACE AND I RENDER YOU HELPLESS. I CANCEL YOUR POWER IN THIS PLACE. IN THE NAME OF JESUS, I PROCLAIM YOU DEAF AND DUMB AND YOU HAVE NO AUTHORITY HERE. YOU ARE BOUND IN THE NAME OF JESUS."

When you use your binding power, immediately begin thanking God and praising Him for the work He has done. Most modern-day Christians have not exercised their binding power over the devil. Instead, they have made committees and have bound men — God's men.

If you are going to spoil a strong man's house, you must first bind him. (Matt. 12:29.) If you are having difficulties with your finances, bind the devil from interfering in your financial affairs. He is illegally trespassing on your property. Get him off right away. After you bind him, begin intercessory prayer and use the power of the Holy Spirit to block his return. You cannot keep birds from flying over your head, but you can keep them from nesting in your hair.

Use the power delegated to you. You are the reason God is in business, to take care of you. He is on your side, not against you. The only way this will work is for you to put it to work. Don't wait until you get in a jam before you pray. If you wait until you are sick before you believe God will heal you, you may as well pack your bags and go to the hospital. The time to believe God for healing is when you are well. Thank God right now that you are well and healed. You can do it because you are!!!

Prayer of Intercession

I exhort therefore, that, first of all, supplications, prayers, INTERCESSIONS, and giving of thanks, be made for all men;

For kings, and for all that are in authority; that we may lead a quiet and peaceable life in all godliness and honesty.

For this is good and acceptable in the sight of God our Savior.
1 Timothy 2:1-3

Intercession means going into the presence of authority on behalf of another. It means getting involved in another person's life. Intercession is a matter of life and death, success and failure, health and sickness. When we pray, we are instructed to pray first of all for our president and the leaders of our great nation. You may say: ''Well, I don't like what he is doing.'' Then pray for him. God did not say to pray just for the leaders we like or agree with. Guns, missles, bombs and planes do not make countries strong. Prayers make countries strong. Commit yourself right now to pray for the leadership of your country, your state and the local government.

Pray for your family and your business associates and those with whom you will come in contact each day. When you pray for another, God intervenes in your behalf too. Intercessory prayer is a spiritual law of faith. YOU MUST DO IT "FIRST OF ALL."

Prayer of Thanksgiving and Praise

In every thing GIVE THANKS: for this is the will of God in Christ Jesus concerning you.

1 Thessalonians 5:16

Enter into his gates with THANKSGIVING, and into his courts with praise: be thankful unto him, and bless his name.

Psalm 100:4

There is an old song that begins:

"If I surveyed all the good things that were sent from above;

If I counted all my blessings in the storehouse of love;

Then I ask for one favor beyond mortal being;

I'm sure that Jesus would grant it, again and again."

As you approach God in prayer, begin to thank Him for the many blessings in your life. As a young Christian, begin early in your prayer life to give God thanks IN everything. Notice that I did not say to thank God FOR all things. Some people have thanked God for car wrecks, cancers, colds and their house burning to the ground. One man said to me: "God burned my house down so that I could learn to appreciate my home. I really thank Him for it because I appreciate my home now more than ever before." God did not burn down that man's house. I am sure he does appreciate his home more than before, but why thank God for something He did not do?

When your feet hit the floor each morning, you should begin to thank God for your health, your strength, your business, your family and all the good things He has blessed you with in your life. The Psalmist said to enter into His gates with **thanksgiving,** and into His courts with **praise.** When

31

you pray, praise God. Tell Him how great he is, how strong He is, how merciful He is and how mighty He is. Here is a prayer of praise:

"FATHER, I ADORE YOU. YOU ARE SO BEAUTIFUL AND MERCIFUL. I PRAISE THE GREATEST NAME THAT HAS EVER CROSSED THE LIPS OF MAN. YOU ARE WONDERFUL AND MIGHTY. YOU ARE MY HEAVENLY FATHER AND I LOVE YOU."

Praying like this will cause a real closeness between you and God. He said that if you would lift Him up He would draw you unto Him. (John 12:32.) God is good; His mercy is everlasting; and His truth will endure forever. Praise Him right now.

Prayer of Dedication and Worship

Many times in our lives we have recited the Lord's Prayer. This great prayer should never be reduced to phraseology or a formula. There are several principles of prayer that Jesus taught us in the "model prayer."

John 9:31 says: *Now we know that God heareth not sinners: but if any man be a worshipper of God, and doeth his will, him he heareth.* The first principle of prayer is worship. True worship of God will be contingent upon our relationship with God. Many people pray every day. However, many prayers go unanswered because there is no relationship with the Father. Most folks are long on prayer and short on worship. The main difference between praise and worship is that praise is usually a vocalization and true worship involves the total man: spirit, soul and body. Many times people gather in a church building and praise vocally but their minds are wandering about, thinking about many other things besides God. True and complete worship will flow from you to God as you have the ability to keep your mind on Him. You see, prayer is more than going to God with our needs, it is worship. People want "things," God wants "us."

One of the most frequent errors in praying is ending a prayer with "if it be Thy will." This is a very serious matter. There are very few times when that phrase can rightfully be used. One of them is in praying a prayer of dedication and consecration. When Jesus prayed in the Garden of Gethsemane, He said: *O my Father, if it be possible, let this cup pass from me: nevertheless NOT AS I WILL, BUT AS THOU WILT* (Matt. 26:39). In the Lord's Prayer, He said: *Thy will be done on earth as it is in heaven* (Matt. 6:10). When you truly submit your will to God you are saying that you want to glorify God rather than yourself. You are saying: "God, I do not desire to be selfish. I will do what You want me to do." I will not tell you that this is an easy thing to do. Many people are very strong willed and it is hard for them to relinquish their will to God's will. However, I exhort you to pray that prayer daily. Dedicate and consecrate your whole life to Jesus Christ. The results will be predictable: SUCCESS IN EVERY AREA OF YOUR LIFE.

But if you need finances or healing for your body or anything else within God's known will, DO NOT PRAY "if it be Thy will"!

Someone asked me: "Well, how do you know what the will of God is?" By reading His Word. When a person dies and leaves a will, that will is a legal document containing his stated wishes or desires. God's Word is His will, His stated wishes or desires. Since the words "testament" and "will" mean the same thing, the "New Testament" is better described as the "New Will." Begin to look at the New Testament as God's will for your life. Therefore, when you pray, begin to pray God's Word back to Him.

For example, suppose you were praying for success in your business. You would study God's Word to learn His will for your financial success, and then you would pray like this:

"FATHER, IN THE NAME OF JESUS, YOUR WORD DECLARES IN 3 JOHN 2 THAT ABOVE ALL THINGS

YOU WANT ME TO PROSPER AND BE IN HEALTH EVEN AS MY SOUL PROSPERS. YOU SAID IN PHILLIPIANS 4:19 THAT YOU WOULD MEET ALL MY NEEDS ACCORDING TO YOUR RICHES IN GLORY BY CHRIST JESUS. ACCORDING TO PSALM 23:1 YOU ARE MY SHEPHERD AND I SHALL NOT WANT. YOU ARE NOT A GOD WHO WOULD LIE. THEREFORE, I COME ON THE BASIS OF YOUR WORD AND ASK YOU TO CAUSE MY BUSINESS TO GROW. GIVE ME CONFI-DENCE, BOLDNESS AND STRENGTH TO DO WHAT IS NECESSARY TO BUILD MY BUSINESS. THANK YOU, FATHER. AMEN.''

Can you see the difference in that prayer and the one that is most commonly prayed: ''FATHER, IF IT BE THY WILL FOR ME TO HAVE A GOOD BUSINESS, I ASK YOU TO HELP ME. IF IT'S NOT YOUR WILL, I WILL JUST STAY AT THE LEVEL I AM RIGHT NOW AND SUFFER FOR YOUR SAKE.''

You don't have to suffer for Jesus' sake, He suffered for your sake. He became poor so you could become rich. He became sick that you would be healed. He died that you could live eternally. Everything that He did, He did for you. That makes you a very special person in the eyes of God. Now begin to love yourself. Commit yourself. Surrender your will to God's will and live in everlasting joy and peace. Remember: *NOT AS I WILL, BUT AS THOU WILT* (Matt. 26:39).

Forgiveness
And when ye stand praying, FORGIVE, if ye have ought against any: that your Father also which is in heaven may forgive you your trespasses.

Mark 11:25

I cannot leave the subject of prayer without sharing this great hindrance to answered prayer. If you carry bitterness or unforgiveness in your heart, God cannot regard your requests. If someone has wronged you, go to that person and tell him that you love him and would like to make amends with him. In your own heart you may feel you are right and he is wrong. That does not matter. You take the first step. You go to him. It may take some time for you to see this work in your life. Just act on faith and on the Word. God will do the rest.

Jesus went on to say in Mark 11:26: *But if ye do not forgive, neither will your Father which is in heaven forgive your trespasses.* When you get to the point in your walk with God that you can unconditionally forgive those who have trespassed against you, you are getting ready to be blessed in every area of your life. Your business will grow. Your marriage will get better. You will sleep sounder. You will live longer and have a healthier life. You will learn to enjoy living. Life is great!

"Don't just look for <u>A</u> church, look for <u>THE</u> church."

— *Dr. Willie J. Malone*

4

Which Church?

Let us not neglect our church duties and meetings, as some people do, but encourage and warn each other, especially now that the day of His coming back again is drawing near.

Hebrews 10:25 LNT

Going to church does not make a person a Christian any more than getting in a garage makes him a car. However, attending church is important. The question is, ''Which church?'' ''How do I pick a church?'' ''What should I look for in a church?'' Not only is going to church important, but it is important where you go to church. Look for a church where the people are happy and joyful, a church that is preaching the uncompromising Word of God, a place where you can get fed spiritually. Look for a church that is Jesus minded and not ''building'' minded or ''program'' minded, one that praises God and exalts the Name of Jesus above all things, one where the people love one another and show it by their actions and words. Check to see whether the church is growing or standing still.

A lady told me recently: ''I sure would like to change churches but I have attended this one all my life and have paid so much money into it, I cannot afford to leave it.'' Obviously, she was starving spiritually, but her ''investment'' was more important than her dividends.

Before you decide which church you will attend, pray earnestly to God. Ask Him to guide you. If you are married, talk it over with your mate. Join hands and pray together. Seek God's perfect will for the right church for you and your family. When you choose the place you desire to join, make yourself available to the pastor. Let him know that you are willing to help the fellowship. If you have a special talent, tell him. Get involved. Be a part of the church. Remember, those people will be looking to you for leadership. You will generate excitement in them. They will become excited too.

5

Wisdom for Prosperity

Many Christians really want prosperity but do not have the wisdom to accomplish it. Some people do not know that it is God's will for them to prosper. Others know that God wants them to enjoy prosperity but have failed to see the importance of using wisdom to attain it.

You need to set goals right now. In Hosea 4:6 God says: *My people are destroyed for lack of knowledge.* Proverbs 29:18 tells us that where there is no vision, the people perish. A person who doesn't have goals, or a vision, will lack motivation and be non-productive.

You need to have specific goals in mind. But you should go one step further: Write your goals, put them in a place where you can read them every day.

WRITE THE VISION, and make it plain upon tables, that he may run that readeth it.

For the vision is yet for an appointed time, but at the end it shall speak, and not lie: though it tarry, wait for it; BECAUSE IT WILL SURELY COME, it will not tarry.

Habakkuk 2:2-3

Just as you have set goals for yourself in your business or career, so also you need to set goals in your walk with God. Have a vision for your friends and family to have a personal relationship with Jesus Christ as you have had. Have a vision for your finances. You may set a goal of having your house paid for in five years. If so, write it down! Keep your vision strong and active. When the devil comes around and tries to steal your vision through circumstances, pressure or a crisis, just go back to your notes and read the vision again. This will give your vision strength.

God's Word gives you the right to prosper in every good work. You already know that He wants you to be prosperous. Now you can believe Him for the wisdom to do it. Do not listen to all the folks around you who say that it can't be done. Furthermore, don't try to obtain prosperity on someone else's faith. You may not go about it exactly as another person did in achieving his goals. That's not important. What is important is the fact that you believe in yourself, in your vision, and in God's plan for your individual life.

God has provided you the ability to prosper in everything you do and wherever you go. But it will not just "fall" on you. Success will not attack you. It takes wisdom, understanding, good judgment and diligence to get the job done. You should always make sure that your goals and visions agree with God's Word. If you will follow the instructions in His Word, He will back it up every time. Get Him so involved in your life that He becomes your number one UPLINE.

Get a pencil right now and finish this sentence: MY GOALS ARE:_____

_____.

Say this aloud:
"FROM THIS DAY ON, I WILL PROSPER IN EVERY-THING I DO. WHEREVER I GO, WHATEVER I SET MY HAND TO DO, I WILL BE SUCCESSFUL AND PROSPEROUS. I WILL LEARN HOW TO OPERATE IN GOD'S WISDOM. HIS WORD IS THE SOURCE OF MY WISDOM. IT IS GOD'S WILL FOR ME TO PROSPER, BUT I REALIZE IT IS CONDITIONAL. I WILL OBEY HIS WORD, BE A GOOD STEWARD AND KNOW THAT PROSPERITY IS PROGRESSIVE. I WILL NOT ALLOW THE ENEMY TO STEAL MY FINANCES ANY MORE. I WILL NOT ALLOW ANYONE TO STEAL MY DREAM,

MY GOALS, MY VISION. I WILL NOT ALLOW MYSELF TO SAY, 'I CAN'T,' OR, 'IT'S IMPOSSIBLE.' WHENEVER ANY OBSTACLE GETS IN MY PATHWAY, I WILL USE THE WORD OF GOD, THE NAME OF JESUS AND THE POWER OF THE HOLY SPIRIT TO CLEAR THE WAY TO SEE MY GOALS, VISIONS AND DREAMS COME TO PASS. I WILL ALWAYS GIVE GOD THE GLORY AND PRAISE FOR MY PROSPERITY. I WILL THANK HIM BEFORE I SEE THE FULL MANIFESTATION OF MY VISION. MY GOD NEVER, NEVER FAILS.''

Now get your Bible and mark Proverbs 4:5-13:

GET SKILLFUL AND GODLY WISDOM, get understanding — discernment, comprehension and interpretation; do not forget, and do not turn back from the words of my mouth.

FORSAKE NOT [WISDOM] and she will keep, defend and protect you; love her and she will guard you.

The beginning of Wisdom is this, get Wisdom — skillful and godly Wisdom! For skillful and godly Wisdom is the principal thing. And with all you have gotten get understanding — discernment, comprehension and interpretation.

PRIZE WISDOM HIGHLY and exalt her, and she will exalt and promote you; SHE WILL BRING YOU TO HONOR when you embrace her.

She shall give to your head a wreath of gracefulness; a crown of beauty and glory will she deliver to you.

Hear, O my son, and receive my sayings, and the years of your life shall be many.

I have taught you in the way of skillful and godly Wisdom [which is comprehensive insight into the ways and purposes of God]; I have led you in paths of uprightness.

When you walk, your steps shall not be hampered — your path will be clear and open; and when you run you shall not stumble.

Take fast hold of instruction, do not let go; guard her, FOR SHE IS YOUR LIFE.

Proverbs 4:5-13 AMP

Notice that God says to get wisdom, to forsake not wisdom, and to prize wisdom. Wisdom will bring honor to you. Wisdom is life to you. There is a difference between knowledge and wisdom. Knowledge is intake, wisdom is output. Wisdom is the correct application of knowledge. If God told us He wanted us to have wisdom, He certainly will not withhold it from us. If you lack wisdom, ask God for it in every affair of your life. (James 1:5.) It gives Him pleasure to give good things to you. (Luke 12:32.) You see, He is God of love and love gives.

6

Tithing and Giving

There are many spiritual laws which God has set in motion that will work for anyone who properly applies them. One such law is the law of giving. Jesus clearly defines it in Luke 6:38: *Give, and it will be given to you; good measure, pressed down, shaken together, running over, they will pour into your lap. For by your standard of measure it will be measured to you in return* (NAS). The basic principle that every truly successful Christian has applied is the law of giving. You will never be successful in your business or as a Christian until you learn to give.

Many people ask me: "How much should I give?" God's Word will give you a starting place.

Bring ye all the tithes into the storehouse, that there may be meat in mine house, and prove me now herewith, saith the Lord of hosts, if I will not open you the windows of heaven, and pour you out a blessing, that there shall not be room enough to receive it.

And I will rebuke the devourer for your sakes, and he shall not destroy the fruits of your ground; neither shall your vine cast her fruit before the time in the field, saith the Lord of hosts.

Malachi 3:10-11

The word tithe means "a tenth." A good starting place and guideline for giving is ten dollars of every one hundred dollars your receive as income. As you learn to operate in this great law, you may find yourself increasing your giving to a larger percentage. Just be obedient. It is impossible to outgive God. He said He would open the windows of heaven and pour you out such blessing you would not have room to receive it.

Find a church that "feeds" you spiritually (that is the storehouse) and begin to tithe through it. Paul told the Corinthians that you reap what you sow. (2 Cor. 9:6.) If you sow bountifully, you will reap bountifully. But if you sow sparingly, you will reap sparingly. If you want the best that God has for you, then give Him your best in tithes, offerings, energy, time and talents. One of the greatest joys you will ever get out of life is being able to give. Some of the wealthiest men on this earth are great givers.

Deuteronomy 8:18 says: *But you shall remember the Lord your God, for IT IS HE WHO IS GIVING YOU POWER TO MAKE WEALTH, that He may confirm His covenant which He swore to your fathers, as it is this day* (NAS).

Why do you suppose that God gives you the power to get wealth? He wants you to be blessed and to bless others. No one can push you up the ladder of success unless you are willing to climb. No one can make you give unless you are willing to give. Begin today! Watch God honor His Word.

7

Your Spiritual House

Dr. Robert Munger has written a masterpiece regarding the heart, the dwelling place of Christ. By permission, I share a portion of it:

One evening I invited Jesus Christ into my heart. What an entrance He made! It was not a spectacular, emotional thing, but very real. Something happened at the very center of my life. He came into the darkness of my heart and banished the chill. He started music where there had been stillness, and He filled the emptiness with His own loving, wonderful fellowship. I have never regretted opening the door to Christ and I never will — not into eternity.

In the joy of this new-found relationship, I said to Jesus Christ, "Lord, I want this heart of mine to be Yours. I want You to settle down here and be perfectly at home. Everything I have belongs to You. Let me show You around."

*The first room was the **study** — the library. In my home, this room of the mind is a very small room with very thick walls, but is a very important room. In a sense, it is the control room of the house. He entered with me and looked around at the books in the bookcase, the magazines on the table, the pictures on the wall. As I followed His gaze, I became uncomfortable.*

Strangely, I had not felt self-conscious about this before, but now that He was there looking at these things, I was embarrassed. Some books were there that His eyes were too pure to behold. There was a lot of trash and literature on the table that a Christian had no business reading, and as for the pictures on the wall — the imaginations and thoughts of the mind — some of these were shameful.

I turned to Him and said, "Master, I know that this room needs some radical alterations. Will You help me make it what it ought to be, and bring every thought into captivity to You?" "Certainly," He said. "First of all, take all the things that you are reading and looking at which are not helpful, pure, good, and true, and throw them out. Now put on the empty shelves the books of the Bible. Fill the library with scripture and 'meditate therein day and night' (Joshua 1:8). As for the pictures on the wall, you will have difficulty controlling these images, but there is an aid." He gave me a full-sized portrait of Himself. "Hang this centrally," He said, "on the wall of the mind."

I did so, and I have discovered through the years that when my attention is centered upon Christ Himself, His purity and power cause impure imaginings to retreat. So He has helped me to bring my thoughts into captivity.

From the study we went into the **dining room**, the room of appetites and desires. I spent a good deal of time here and put forth much effort in satisfying my wants. I said to Him, "This is a very big room, and I am quite sure You will be pleased with what we serve." He seated Himself at the table with me and asked, "What is on the menu for dinner?" "Well," I said, "my favorite dishes: old bones, corn husks, sour garbage, leeks, onions, and garlic right out of Egypt." These were the things I liked — worldly fare.

When the food was placed before Him, He said nothing, but I observed that He did not eat it. I said to Him, "Master, You don't care for this food? What is the trouble?" He answered, "I have meat to eat that ye know not of . . . If you want food that really satisfies, seek the *will of the Father, not your own pleasures, not your own desires, not your own satisfaction, but seek to please Me. That food will satisfy you.'' There at the table He gave me a taste of the joy of doing God's will. What flavor! What nourishment and vitality it gives to the soul! There is no food like it in all the world. It alone satisfies.*

*From the dining room we walked into the **drawing room**. This room was intimate and comfortable. I liked it. It had a fireplace, upholstered chairs, a sofa, and a quiet atmosphere. He said, ''This is indeed a delightful room. Let us come here often. It is secluded and quiet, and we can have fellowship together.'' Well, as a young Christian I was thrilled. I could not think of anything I would rather do that have a few minutes apart with Christ in intimate fellowship. He promised, ''I will be here early every morning. Meet Me here, and we will start the day together.'' So, morning after morning, I would come downstairs to the drawing room, or ''withdrawing room,'' as I liked to think of it. He would take a book of the Bible from the case. We would open it and read together. He would tell me of its richness and unfold to me its truths. My heart warmed as He revealed the love and the grace He had toward me. These were wonderful hours. Little by little, under the pressure of many responsibilities, the time began to be shortened. Why, I don't know, but I thought I was too busy to spend time with Christ. This was not intentional, you understand. It just happened that way. Finally, not only was the time shortened, but I began to miss a day now and then. Perhaps it was some other pressing need. I would miss it two days in a row and oftentimes more. I remember one morning when I was rushing downstairs, eager to be on my way, that I passed the drawing room and noticed that the door was ajar. Looking in, I saw a fire in the fireplace and the Master sitting there. Suddenly in dismay I thought to myself, ''He is my guest. I invited Him into*

my heart! He has come and yet I am neglecting Him.''
With downcast glance, I said, ''Blessed Master, forgive
me. Have You been here all these mornings?'' ''Yes,'' He
said, ''I told you I would be here every morning to meet
with you. Remember, I love you. I have redeemed you at
great cost. I desire your fellowship. Even if you cannot
keep the quiet time for your own sake, do it for Mine.''

Don't let Christ wait alone in the drawing room of
your heart, but every day find time, when, with your
Bible and in prayer, you may have fellowship with Him.

He asked me if I had a **playroom.** I was hoping He
would not ask me about this. There were certain associations and friendships, activities, and amusements that I
wanted to keep for myself. One evening when I was
leaving to join some college companions, He stopped me
with a glance and asked, ''Are you going out this
evening?'' I replied, ''Yes.'' ''Good,'' He said, ''I would
like to go with you.'' ''Oh,'' I answered rather
awkwardly, ''I don't think, Lord Jesus, that You would
really want to go with me. Let's go out tomorrow night.
Tomorrow night we will go to prayer meeting, but tonight
I have another appointment.'' ''I'm sorry,'' He said, ''I
thought that when I came into your home, we were going
to do everything together, to be partners. I want you to
know that I am willing to go with you.'' ''Well,'' I
mumbled, slipping out the door, ''We will go someplace
tomorrow night.'' That evening I spent some miserable
hours. I felt wretched. What kind of friend was I to Christ
when I was deliberately leaving Him out of my
associations, doing things and going places that I knew
very well He would not enjoy? When I returned that
evening, there was a light in His room, and I went up to
talk it over with Him. I said, ''Lord, I have learned my
lesson. I cannot have a good time without You. We will do
everything together.'' Then we went down into the
playroom of the house and He transformed it. He brought

new friends into my life, new satisfactions, new lasting joys. Laughter and music have been ringing through the house ever since.

One day I found Him waiting for me at the door. There was an arresting look in His eye, and He said to me as I entered, "There is a peculiar odor in the house. Something is dead around here. It is upstairs. I am sure it is in the hall cupboard." As soon as He said the words, I knew what He was talking about. Yes, there was a small hall cupboard up there on the landing, just a few feet square. In that cupboard, behind lock and key, I had one or two little personal things that I did not want Christ to see. I knew they were dead and rotting things, and I wanted them so for myself that I was afraid to admit they were there. I went up with Him, and as we mounted the stairs the odor became stronger and stronger. He pointed to the door. I was angry. That's the only way I can put it. I had given Him access to the library, the dining room, the drawing room, the playroom, and now He was asking me about a little two-by-four cupboard. I said inwardly, "This is too much. I am not going to give Him the key." Reading my thoughts, He said, "If you think I am going to stay up here on the second floor with this odor, you are mistaken. I will go out on the porch." I saw Him start down the stairs. My resistance collapsed. When one comes to know and love Christ, the worst thing that can happen is to sense His companionship withdrawing. I had to surrender. "I will give You the key," I said sadly, "But You will have to open up the cupboard and clean it out. I haven't the strength to do it." "Just give Me the key," He said. "Authorize Me to take care of that cupboard and I will." With trembling fingers, I passed the key to Him. He took it, walked over to the door, opened it, entered, took out all the putrefying stuff that was rotting there, and threw it away. Then He cleaned the cupboard and painted it. It was done in a moment. Oh, what victory and release to have that dead thing out of my life!

Complete Lordship

A thought came to me. "Lord, is there any chance that You would take over the management of the whole house and operate it for me as You did that cupboard? Would You take the responsibility to keep my life what it ought to be?" His face lighted up as He replied, "Certainly, that is what I want to do. You cannot be a victorious Christian in your own strength. Let Me do it through you and for you. That is the way." "But," He added slowly, "I am just a guest. I have no authority to proceed, since the property is not Mine." Dropping to my knees, I said, "Lord, You have been a guest and I have been the host. From now on I am going to be the servant. You are going to be the Lord." Running as fast as I could to the strongbox, I took out the title deed to the house describing its properties, assets, and liabilities. I eagerly signed the house over to Him alone for time and eternity. "Here," I said. "Here it is, all that I am and have, forever. Now You run the house. I'll just remain with You as a servant and friend." Things are different since Jesus Christ has settled down and has made His home in my heart.*

In Conclusion

God's Word declares that you cannot serve two masters. This does not mean that you will never sin or have a "dirty room" in your house. Just be honest with God. Ask Him to show you where you are weak and He will turn those weaknesses into strengths. It is not a shame to have a weakness. It is a shame to have a weakness and not admit it.

---

* Excerpt from *My Heart — Christ's Home* by Robert Munger, copyright 1954 by Inter-Varsity Christian Fellowship of the U.S.A. and used by permission of Inter-Varsity Press, Downers Grove, IL 60515.

So, check your "spiritual house." Be very cautious what you read and watch on television. Don't clutter your mind with garbage. Computer programmers have a saying: GI-GO (Garbage In — Garbage Out). Be careful what you see, hear and where you go.

Colossians 3:17 says: *And whatsoever ye do in word or deed, do all in the name of the Lord Jesus.* Don't try to clean everybody else's house. Concentrate on keeping your house clean. Remember, it takes time to clean the house. Don't get impatient. House cleaning is an everyday event. If you think you cannot do. it, you have just passed the first test. You cannot do it by yourself. Ask Jesus Christ to help you. Learn to enjoy living a Christian life. IT IS FUN.

8

Saying Right Words

How forcible are right WORDS.

Job 6:25

Death and life are in the power of the TONGUE.

Proverbs 18:21

My son, attend to my WORDS; incline thine ear unto my sayings.

Let THEM not depart from thine eyes; keep THEM in the midst of thine heart.

For THEY are life unto those that find THEM, and health to all their flesh.

Proverbs 4:20-22

For verily I say unto you, That whosoever SHALL SAY unto this mountain, Be thou removed, and be thou cast into the sea; and shall not doubt in his heart, but shall believe that those things which HE SAITH shall come to pass; HE SHALL HAVE WHATSOEVER HE SAITH.

Mark 11:23

Your words can change your life. Power is released through your mouth. How many times have you said something like this? "Every time I wash my car it rains!" Or: "Why does everything always happen to me?" Or: "It's no use, I'll never make it!"

Once a young lady came into my office and asked me: "Dr. Malone, you don't need anybody to work for you, do you?"

I said, "No, but if I did I would not consider you unless you change your attitude."

Now why did I answer her that way? Because she approached me with a negative statement that revealed her negative attitude. I proceeded to teach her the importance of right words. When she left my office, she was smiling and confident. She learned what everyone should learn: YOU CAN TRAIN YOUR WORDS TO BE FAITH WORDS, LOVE WORDS, PLEASING WORDS, AND POSITIVE WORDS. Begin to be word-conscious.

Tell the Truth

I have noted for some time that many people, even Christians, are not honest. If you ask them if they will come to a business meeting, they will say: "I'll try, I am hoping I can make it." That is what you hear. But inside they have no intention of coming. The reason they are not honest with you is they don't want to hurt your feelings by saying: "No, I cannot (or don't want to) come to the meeting."

If you tell a person that you are going to go to a meeting, GO TO THE MEETING! If you know you cannot attend that particular night, then tell him you will not be there. BE HONEST! I have never seen a dishonest person succeed in business for any period of time. Your word should be your bond. Proverbs 15:4 says: *A wholesome tongue is a tree of life.* Make sure that your tongue is wholesome. Tell the truth.

Words Release Faith

Don't ever let the devil tell you that you do not have faith. You do. You have all the faith you need. You don't need 15 tons of faith to get the job done. All you need to know is how to release the faith you already have. You could have an over abundance of faith, but unless you knew how to release it, you may as well not have it. It's like having $100,000 in the bank and not knowing how to write a check. You could die in poverty. You must learn to draw from your heavenly bank account. In releasing your faith, the mouth is the dominant factor.

Remember this spiritual law: YOU CAN HAVE WHAT YOU SAY. This law works in the positive and the negative realm. You can make this law work for you or against you. It is your choice.

Suppose you are struggling in your business, just barely making it, and someone asks you: "Hey, how are you doing in the soap business?" If you reply, "Oh, I just don't know how in the world I can ever make this business go. My wife won't help me, my friends call me 'Soapy,' and this whole town is weird. I'm going to just give this whole thing up in a few days and quit!" then YOU JUST GOT HUNG BY YOUR TONGUE! Be positive! Say something like this instead: "This is the greatest business in the world. I am not where I want to be yet but, thank God, I'm not where I used to be. God and I are partners, I cannot fail. I am having fun. You should take a close look at this business. It's great! Have a good day." Can you see the difference? Guard your mouth.

If your wife asks you, "Honey, don't you ever get discouraged and want to quit and sit down and watch Monday Night Football?" tell her: "No way! I am going to help others succeed and in the meantime we will succeed."

Wives, let me give you a word of wisdom: ENCOURAGE YOUR HUSBAND. TALK POSITIVE AROUND HIM. IF YOU DETECT ANY WEARINESS, TELL HIM HE CAN DO IT AND THAT YOU HAVE CONFIDENCE IN HIM. It is like a shot in the arm. He will grit his teeth, bow his neck, set his jaw, put his hand to the wheel and keep going.

God's Word says that He will never leave you nor forsake you. He is with you at all times to help you. Allow Him to do it by saying right words.

9

Confession Brings Possession

We cannot reduce Almighty God's power to mere formulas. Just because you "say it" does not bring automatic possession. I would be foolish to tell you that **all** you have to do is confess and possess. You must believe, forgive, obey God's Word and live a life that is pleasing to our Heavenly Father. However, God's creative power will work for you if you will confess His Word daily. You should say the same things that God says about you. Agree with God's Word and it will work for you. Here are some guidelines to confession. Allow these to be carved inside you. Don't wait until you are in poverty before you confess God's Word about prosperity. Don't wait until you are sick before you confess that God will heal you. Prepare now! Read these aloud daily as your confession:

For Fears and Worry:
1 Cor. 12:14-27: **I am the body of Christ and Satan has no power over me.**
Romans 12:21: **I overcome evil with good.**
1 John 4:4: **Greater is He that is in me than he that is in the world.**
Psalm 23:4: **I will fear no evil for You are with me, Lord. Your Word and Your Spirit comfort me.**
Isaiah 54:14: **I am far from oppression and fear does not come near me.**
Isaiah 54:17: **No weapon that is formed against me shall prosper, for my righteousness is of the Lord.**
Psalm 1:3: **Whatsoever I do shall prosper for I am like a tree planted by rivers of water.**

Galatians 1:4: **Lord, You have delivered me from the evils of this world for that is Your will.**

Psalm 91:10: **No evil will befall me, neither shall any plague come near my dwelling.**

Psalm 91:11: **Lord, You have given Your angels charge over me, to keep me in all my ways.**

Proverbs 12:28: **In my pathway is life and there is no death.**

James 1:25: **I am a doer of the Word of God, and am blessed in my deeds.**

Ephesians 6:16: **I take the shield of faith and stop everything the enemy brings against me.**

Galatians 3:13: **Christ has redeemed me from the curse of the law. I forbid any kind of curse to come on me.**

Revelation 12:11: **I overcome the enemy by the blood of Christ and the word of my testimony.**

James 4:7: **The devil flees from me because I resist him in Jesus' Name.**

Psalm 119:89: **Your Word, O God, is forever settled in heaven.**

Isaiah 54:13: **Great is the peace of my children for they are taught of the Lord.**

For Material and Physical Needs:

Galatians 3:13: **Christ has redeemed me from the curse of the law, from poverty, sickness and death, and they shall not come upon me.** (See Deut. 28.)

2 Cor. 8:9: **For poverty, the Lord has given me wealth.**

Isaiah 53:4-5: **For sickness, He has given me health.**

Psalm 119:25: **It is true unto me according to the Word of God.**

Psalm 37:4: **I delight myself in the Lord and He gives me the desires of my heart.**

Luke 6:38: **I have given and it is given unto me —** **pressed down, shaken together, running over.**

2 Cor. 9:8: **I have all sufficiency of all things and abound to all good works.**

Phil. 4:19: **I lack nothing for my God supplies all my needs according to His riches.**

Psalm 23:1: **The Lord is my Shepherd; I DO NOT WANT.**

For Guidance and Wisdom:

John 16:13: **The Spirit of truth abides in me and teaches me all things. He guides me into all truth.**

Proverbs 3:5-6: **I trust in the Lord with all my heart and lean not to my own understanding. In all my ways I acknowledge Him and He directs my path.**

Psalm 119:105: **The Word of God is a lamp unto my feet and a light unto my path.**

Psalm 138:8: **I am not troubled about what to do for the Lord perfects that which concerns me.**

Colossians 3:16: **I let the Word of Christ dwell in me richly in all wisdom.**

John 10:2-5: **I follow the good Shepherd for I know His voice; a stranger I will not follow.**

Romans 12:2: **I am not conformed to this world, but I am transformed by renewing my mind by the Word of God.**

For Comfort and Strength:

Nehemiah 8:10: **The joy of the Lord is my strength.**

Psalm 27:1: **The Lord is the strength of my life.**

1 John 4:4: **Greater is He that is in me than he that is in the world.**

Proverbs 4:21-22: **I will not let the Word depart from before my eyes, for it is life and health.**

Ephesians 4:29: **I let no corrupt words come out of my mouth but that which is good to edifying.**

Ephesians 4:27: **I refuse to give place to the devil.**

Ephesians 4:15: **I speak the truth in love and grow up into Christ in all things.**

John 10:28: **He gives me eternal life and no man shall pluck me out of His hand.**

Colossians 3:15: **I let the peace of God rule in my heart. I refuse to be worried about anything.**

Matthew 16:19: **That which I refuse to allow here, God also refuses to allow; and that which I do allow, God also allows to come to pass here on earth.**

Mark 16:17-18: **I am a believer and these signs shall follow me. I take authority over the devil; I speak with new tongues; I lay hands on the sick, and they recover.**

Colossians 2:10: **I am complete in Him who is the head of all principality and power.**

DEVELOP AN IMAGE OF YOURSELF AS YOU SAY THIS:
*Thank You, Father, I'm an heir. I'm a joint-heir with
    Jesus Christ.*
I have the mind of Christ.
I have the wisdom of Christ.
I have the ability of Christ.
I have His health.
As He is in heaven, so am I upon the earth.
I can do all things through Christ who strengthens me.
*My God shall supply all my needs according to His riches
    in glory by Christ Jesus.*
The Greater One abides within me.
*And no circumstances — no situation — nothing can come
    against me and overtake me:*
    No sickness,
    No anxiety,
    No fear,
    No worry.
    *No financial burden can come against me and overtake
        me.*
Neither can anything overtake me in my mind.
*Because greater is He that is in me that he that is in the
    world.*

I've renewed my mind and will renew my mind
By the Word of the Living God, and it shall cause me to
prosper
In every area of my life.
And I will be a living epistle of the Living Christ —
read and known of all men.
Hallelujah.
And the world will see in me Jesus
In all of His power
In all of His glory
Because I'm being changed
Day by day
From glory to glory.
Hallelujah.
Because Jesus lives in me, I'm a lovely person.
Because Jesus lives in me, I'm a joyful person.
Because Jesus lives in me, I'm a peaceful person.
Because Jesus lives in me, I'm a patient person.
Because Jesus lives in me, I'm a gentle person.
Because Jesus lives in me, I'm a good person.
Because Jesus lives in me, I'm a meek person.
Because Jesus lives in me, I'm a faithful person.
Because Jesus lives in me, I'm a temperate person.

(Scripture references: Rom. 8:17; 1 Cor. 2:16; 1 Cor. 1:30;
John 14:12; Is. 53:4-5; 1 John 4:17; Phil. 4:13; Phil. 4:19;
1 John 4:4; Rom. 12:2; Ps. 1:1-3; 2 Cor. 3:2-3, 3:18, 4:7, 5:17,
5:21.)

10
Living Happily Ever After

Although the title of this chapter is the well-known closing for happy-ending fairy tales, it can also be a reality in your life. Life is so beautiful. We live in the greatest era of all times. However, there are some people who think that this world is bad and getting worse. For this reason, they sit around wishing their life away. They want to hurry and get to heaven so they can get out of this "mess." Don't ever become destination-oriented. Always be journey-oriented. It is perfectly in order to have goals and visions and you should work toward them. But learn to live one day at a time and enjoy it. Yesterday is today's memory and tomorrow is today's dream.

You might say: "Yes, but you don't know how many defeats I have experienced." Turn those defeats into victories, trials into triumphs, and learn to salvage something from setback. You are not the only one who has ever experienced defeat. If the devil can convince you that you are a loser, you will never be a winner. Just because you fail doesn't mean you are a failure. Now hold your head up and look the world straight in the eye and say: "LOOK OUT, WORLD, HERE COMES A WINNER!" Get the drift?

The Happy Home

Don't ever let anyone steal your dream. You and your marriage partner can accomplish anything you can agree upon. That is why I share some tips on marriage with you.

Always keep communications open between you and your spouse. If you cannot talk together, you cannot live together. When an argument or disagreement develops, analyze it to determine its origin and what triggered it. If a word did it, don't use that word again. Find out what is offensive to your mate and avoid it. Try to bring out the best in your spouse. Encourage him or her to do what they do best. Never go to sleep angry with each other.

Husbands, remember that you may have more physical energy than your wife. Help her with her household chores. Do as many things as possible together. Worship and pray together. Make an effort to do nice things for one another. Avoid situations where sin and lust might creep in. Don't ever refuse each other intimate love. Be alert for things that will help your mate to grow spiritually. Be ready at all times to forgive one another. Don't bring up a point of disagreement or a problem once it is forgiven. When you forgive, forget. And above all, be thankful for each other and express your gratitude to each other.

If you have a family, begin to develop togetherness. Fifteen hundred school children were asked the question: "What do you think makes a happy family?" The most frequent answer was doing things together. IT IS NOT SO MUCH WHAT WE DO **FOR** OUR CHILDREN THAT MATTERS AS IT IS WHAT WE DO **WITH** THEM. Make family time a top priority. Evaluate your present family times and begin to plan how to make them more enriching.

"Family Nights" are very important. One night each week plan a time to study the Bible as a family. Allow each family member an opportunity to be a leader in the study. If your children are very young, get a Bible storybook or devotional book and make this time of study lots of fun. Plan recreational times together. It is true that the family that prays together stays together. But it is also true that the family that **plays** together stays together.

One of the most enjoyable times at our house is the dinner meal in the evening. Never use this time to discipline, for negative talk, or to criticize the people you have come in contact with that day. Father, Mother, do not dominate the conversation. Allow the children time to tell the exciting things that happened to them that day. Share your excitement with them. If you have had some interesting experience at work, share it with the family. You see, you can live happily ever after. But it takes effort on your part. God has given you the ingredients for a heaven on earth. It's up to you to cultivate that earthly Garden of Eden. IT IS YOUR FAMILY. Don't ever forget that.

Ten Commandments for Husbands

1. **Thou shalt provide the necessities of life for thy family, and shalt not close thy fist too tightly around thy billfold.**
2. **Remember that thou must assume the responsibility of thy home.**
3. **Thou shalt share some of thy recreation hours with thy wife and family, remembering that a family which plays together stays together.**
4. **Thou shalt take thy wife into thy confidence and share thy plans with her, remembering that she is thy partner, not thy hired hand.**
5. **Thou shalt enter into thy house with cheerfulness and avoid faultfinding and a critical spirit as much as possible.**
6. **Thou shalt not embarrass or criticize thy wife before thy friends and relatives; nor shalt thou allow anyone to criticize thy wife to thy face and get away with it.**
7. **Thou shalt not take thy wife for granted, but shalt keep her love in the same way in which thou didst win it.**
8. **Thou shalt live a life of high moral purity.**
9. **Thou shalt have no one before thy wife except God.**
10. **Thou shalt give God a place — yea, first place — in thy heart and home.**

Ten Commandment for Wives

1. **Thou shalt not nag.**
2. **Thou shalt spend thy husband's money with care and wisdom.**
3. **Thou shalt keep thy tongue with all diligence, not permitting it to run loose in gossip.**
4. **Thou shalt not compare thy husband with other men, nor shalt thou remind him of all the men thou couldst have married.**
5. **Thou shalt not be the boss.**
6. **Thou shalt not possess an excessively jealous spirit.**
7. **Thou shalt coddle thy husband, doing for him those little things that mean so much.**
8. **Thou shalt give diligence to keep thyself and thy home attractive, remembering thou must not only win thy husband's love, but also keep it.**
9. **Thou shalt prize thy womanly virtues and value them more than life itself.**
10. **Thou shalt have a genuine relationship, faith and trust in God.**

When God created man, He said it was not good for him to be alone. Therefore, He made woman. God said that she would be man's helpmeet. In other words, ladies, you should help meet the needs of your husband. God also said that a man should leave his father and mother and cleave to his wife. The word "cleave" means to never stop chasing. Husbands, love your wives. Remember how you chased her before you were married? Take your wife out on a date. Hold her hand, look her in the eyes and tell her you love her. Then brace yourself. You will live happily ever after!

Summary

If you bought a new automobile, you would read the manual for directions on the care and maintenance of it. My prayer is that this book can be a manual or guide whereby you may not let your decision to become a Christian be the end, but rather a new beginning. Step One was truly a giant step for you. You feel good about your decision. A thousand-mile journey begins with a single step. You have made that step. But don't stop. Step Two is important. See you at the top! We all love you. YA-HOO!